Children & Prayer

Is Prayer with children an intentional discipline
or does it just happen?

Penelope Allen White

CONTENTS

ACKNOWLEDGEMENT

Thanks be to God, my personal Savior Jesus Christ, and the Holy Spirit. Expressions of sincere thanks are offered to: my husband B.R. WHITE, sons DARIUS, CEDRIC, family, friends, church family, many prayer partners, various editors/ readers, and Xulon Publishers. I am especially grateful for: my home church family, Rising Sun Missionary Baptist Church (Hernando, Mississippi), all of my Pastors, Sunday School teachers, and Christians who nurtured me in the faith and in the practice of prayer; The Ebenezer AME Church Family, Cornerstone AME Church Family, St. Mark AME Church Family, and St. Paul United Methodist Church Family; Temple of Praise; Center for the Ministry of Teaching Virginia Seminary; Professors and staff of Virginia Seminary and Howard University School of Divinity.

DEDICATION

This book/project is dedicated to the memory of my parents Mr. and Mrs. William Parker Allen, Sr. (Augusta) and all of my ancestors who faithfully prayed for me. It is also dedicated to my husband B.R. White, sons Darius E. and Cedric R., and all the praying generations yet to be born.

INTRODUCTION

For many years, prayer has been the subject of numerous books, studies, and discussions in the Christian life. It is one of the most important disciplines for individuals who desire to have a personal relationship with God through the Lord Jesus Christ. Christ Himself exemplified the importance of prayer by engaging in prayer as a lifestyle. The Holy Scriptures record countless prayers that were prayed to God the Father by His own son Jesus. Jesus would often get up early in the morning, seek time to be alone with God, and pray (Mark 1:35).

Prayer may be defined as communion with God. Why do you think Jesus prayed? When did He pray? Where did He pray? How did He pray? Jesus teaches us what He learned and that is prayer must be a priority in our lives. He needed and wanted to be in intimate conversation with His Father. Jesus understood that in order to know what pleased the Father, He would have to hear His words, instructions, and plans. All of these come through praying to God. Jesus was given power to do miracles and many great things. All of which were made possible through His prayer life. Jesus' followers recognized the vital part prayer was to Jesus' ministry and so they asked Him to teach them to pray. Prayer is an instrument for change and often the change is in the one who prays. Prayer connects you to your true self and it goes directly to the Source. Prayer allows us to commune with the Creator, Master of the universe, The Almighty. In meaningful and effective communication, there is an appropriate time to be silent, listen, talk, laugh, and cry.

As followers of Christ, we do well to imitate His model in the discipline of developing a consistent prayer life. Jesus didn't just teach or talk about prayer, but rather He did it. He prayed on many occasions and demonstrated to us how to enter into the presence of God Almighty. Some circumstances were times of giving thanks, crisis, or decision-making. Sometimes it was after ministering to multitudes, Jesus sought the solitude of personal time in prayer with His Father. Jesus' on going ministry and entire life was under girded and saturated with consistent prayer. As followers of Christ, our lives must be as His. God was Jesus' Source of strength, power, and wisdom and these were realized through prayer. Prayer is entering into face-to-face communication with God. The Old Testament records for us many conversation between God and God's chosen servants (i.e. God and Abraham-Genesis 15 and 17; God and Moses-Exodus 3,4, and 6; God and Noah-Genesis 6,7,8, and 9).

Prayer is more than a pious ceremony or formality. When offered in sincerity, faith, truth, and trust, prayer has a transforming effect on our lives. When Jesus went to the mountaintop with His disciples Peter, James, and John, as Jesus prayed the appearance of His face was altered and His robe became white and glistening (Luke 9:29). Jesus was transformed right before the disciples eyes. When we pray earnestly, we are on a path to have our lives taken over by God and to be changed. That is to say our destiny is changed because of prayer. Though the disciples did not understand all of what was occurring, it was very obvious that something very significant was happening. This special something, this transformation, this defining moment was directly related to prayer.

God's will is identified and revealed through prayer and this transforms our will and changes our destiny, not always instantaneously, but as a life forming experience. As Jesus approached crucifixion, during prayer He was able to overcome His agony and agree with the perfect will of His Father God. This is clearly expressed when He is able to pray "Father, if you are willing, take this cup from me; nevertheless, not my will but Your will be done" (Luke 22:42). Prayer is essential to us, as it was to Christ, in order for us know and follow the will of God. In this way, God's power is released to us and our destiny is changed as we pray to the Father through Jesus the Son.

God's heart is wide open to prayer and His Son Jesus is the door. We are no longer barred from nearness with God, but we can now enter through the door of God's grace and mercy because of Jesus Christ. *Can we be taught how to pray?* To be prayers to God we must be lovers of God. Real prayer and communication come from love and we are grateful to be invited into the heart of love.

When children can be taught the effectiveness and importance of the power behind prayer because of the One to Whom we pray, perhaps they will understand that their prayers are directed to the ultimate power in the entire universe. Many prayers from the Bible affected the destiny of individuals and nations. Praying that results in lives that are changed forever is worth teaching to children. A few PRAYERS THAT CHANGED LIVES are:

Genesis 32: 9-12

Jacob prayed, "O God of my father Abraham, God of my father Issac, O Lord who said to me, 'Go back to your country and your relatives, and I will make you prosper'. I am unworthy of all the kindness and faithfulness you have shown your servant. I had only my staff when I crossed this Jordan, but now I have become two groups. Save me, I pray, from the hand of my brother Esau, for I am afraid he will come and attack me, and also the mothers with their children. But you have said, 'I will surely make you prosper and will make your descendants like the sand of the sea, which cannot be counted.'"

Jacob's life had been one of turmoil and strife even from the time he and his twin brother were in their mother's womb; yet, God had a perfect plan for his life. He was known by his character, Jacob the name meaning trickster/schemer. After having been separated from his family, cheated by his uncle Laban, tricked into marrying someone he did not want, laboring 14 years to marry the woman he really loved, Jacob still has the favor of God Almighty. His prayer reveals his fears; thus, we can be honest with God in prayer. Pouring out our deepest feelings to a God Who already knows everything there is to know about us and yet cares so lovingly. With God, our past does not determine our destiny. God's love for us is truly amazing!

God's love began in creation-He prepared a world for us-He created mankind for fellowship. When man sinned, God provided for him by giving a covering. HE LOVED US WITH A CROSS! God's love is everlasting/eternal. God's love is unconditional-we can do nothing that warrants Him loving us-IT'S WHAT HE DID! His love is far reaching-to the uttermost. His love is irresistible. Jacob reminded God of His promise. We have been taught that God is moved by His Word. As we pray back to God what God has spoken to us, we align ourselves with His Word/will. God is bound by His word, not our crying and pleading (though sometimes we do). God is not a man that He should lie so once He gives His Word He performs. Jacob recalls that God is the God of His fathers acknowledging that he and his family have a history with God. When we share with our children, grandchildren, and others, we say that this God we serve is the true and living God. He has been God for ages and ages and He is still God. God's love for us is truly amazing!

Genesis 20:

Abraham who was God's chosen for fear of his life told Abimelech King of Gerar that Sarah was his sister. The king took her, but God appeared to him in a dream one night and declared him to be as good as dead because he had taken a married woman. God had closed the wombs of the King's wife and servant girls. Though the king appealed to God because he didn't know Sarah was Abraham's wife, God said return her and my prophet Abraham will pray for you and you will live. The Bible tells us that after the confession of Abraham to Abimelech and Abimelech's generosity to Abraham, Abraham prayed to God. Abimelech, his wife, and the slave girls were all healed so that they could have children. What a change in destiny! If Abraham had not prayed for Abimelech his progeny would have been non-existent. Though his specific prayer word for word is not written for us, we know that Abraham prayed and God responded. This speaks to me on the importance of praying when God instructs you for whomever he directs me to pray for. We don't always realize what's in the balance, it could be life/

death/entire nation/health/deliverance/salvation. When we pray as directed by God's Spirit (who knows what we should pray), destinies can be changed, lives can be spared, restoration and deliverance can take place. Several years ago, the Lord directed me to wake every morning around 4 AM and pray specifically for my husband. During the summer of 2000, my husband got up early one morning to use the bathroom. Because the Spirit had disciplined me to awaken, I realized he had not returned to bed after several minutes. When I went to check on him, he was slumped over unable to speak or move. I immediately laid hands on him thanked God for sparing his life and called 911. God answers prayer and I am so grateful that He is a prayer hearing and prayer answering God! PRAISE GOD!

Genesis 25:21

Issac and Rebekah had no children and it would seem their destiny was to be childless; yet, Issac prayed to the Lord on behalf of his wife Rebekah and she became pregnant with twins who would become two nations of people. Within our prayer lies the potential for great things to take place. The course of history can be altered by the God we serve when we who are called by His name will humble ourselves, seek His face, and turn from our wicked ways, and pray.

Joshua 7:7

God had given specific instructions regarding the plunder from Ai. Achan acted unfaithfully by stealing the devoted things and hiding them with his own possessions. Although Joshua didn't know this, he did know some sin had been committed because the Lord allowed Israel's enemies to defeat them. Joshua prayed, "O Sovereign Lord, why did you ever bring this people across the Jordan to deliver us into the hands of the Amorites to destroy us? If only we had been content to stay on the other side of the Jordan! O, Lord what can I say, now that Israel has been routed by its enemies? The Canaanites and the other people of the country will hear about this and surround us and wipe out our name from the earth. What then will you do for your own great name?"

When Joshua prayed, God gave very detailed instructions as to how to determine the problem/guilty person. In our seeking the Lord, He reveals specifically the area, situation, or person that needs to be dealt with and the how. God is a God of specificity. He does not deal in vagueness. When God points out sin in our lives, it is very clear what displeases Him and He demands our confronting that and eliminating that thing. God deals with me in the area of demonstrating His love especially to those who attempt to undermine me or scheme against me.

He reveals the plot or scheme then reminds me to love as He does. What a challenge on my own/within myself! Yet, with God's help I'm learning that I can do all things through Christ which strengthens me. THANKS BE TO GOD!

Judges 6: 36-40

God had chosen Gideon to be the leader of Israel; however, Gideon was not convinced. He was fearful and he doubted. He prayed, "If you will save Israel by my hand as you have promised, look, I place a wool fleece on the threshing floor. If there is dew only on the fleece and all the ground is dry, then I will know that you will save Israel by my hand, as you said." That is what happened, Gideon rose early the next day; he squeezed the fleece and wrung out the dew-a bowlful of water. Then Gideon said to God, "Do not be angry with me. Let me make just one more request. Allow me one more test with the fleece. This time make the fleece dry and the ground covered with dew". That night God did so. Only the fleece was dry; all the ground was covered with dew.

Chapter I

Prayer is an essential discipline in the development of faith; therefore, it is important to better understand the ways in which persons learn to pray. Prayer has been recognized as an effective way to revolutionize, transform, and enhance the Christian lifestyle. Prayer can and does include many factors. For this reason it can not be narrowed to simple formulas; however, it is so foundational to Christian growth, some general framework is necessary. Prayer can be defined as an intimate, face-to-face conversation between God and human beings. It is both listening to and talking with God. Prayer is an expression of worship, of love for, and dependence on God. It is a yearning to be near God, which is to say, to experience God's presence. What can sometimes begin as an awkward routine proves to be a rewarding privilege and even a delight, this is prayer.

It has been my experience that some children pray very readily and others admit that they do not pray nor know how to pray. This matter intrigued me and I became more curious as to how do children who know the practice of prayer learn to pray and could those children who do not pray learn the art. During the many years that I have worked with children, their parents, Church school teachers, and others who have influenced the lives of children, I believe that those relationships have a significant impact on children's learning pattern as it relates to prayer.

This study grew out of my work with children and observing the desire children have expressed to be instructed in the area of prayer.

My personal desire to expand my prayer life, initiate the development of at least three new prayer teams, and experience the joy of having others know the power of prayer were the precursors to this study.

One of the purposes of this book is to examine the question of how children learn to pray as an intentional discipline. Thus as a learned activity, what methods are used to teach children to pray? A second purpose is to determine for whom and for what do children most often pray? Thirdly, since prayer consists of various types including adoration, confession, thanksgiving, and supplications (ACTS), which type prayers do children most often pray? A fourth purpose is to compare some methods people use when working with children to enhance their prayer life as followers of Christ.

Chapter II

Children are a heritage from the Lord entrusted to us for the purposes of teaching, training and nurturing them in the ways of God so that their lives would bring glory to Him. God's laws and miraculous answers to prayer are to passed on from one generation to the next. Each child has been created with a specific destiny in the mind of God. In other words, each is a one-of-a-kind Master's design crafted specifically for God's special purpose. God's name is taken into the future by them.

As followers of Christ, we help children learn to imitate His model in the discipline of developing a consistent prayer life. Jesus didn't just teach or talk about prayer, but rather He did it. He prayed on many occasions and demonstrated to us how to enter into the presence of God.[1]

Can children be taught how to pray? Children seem to have a great capacity to be open and honest which is one of main components of prayer. There should be no pretense, only honesty in prayer. Children usually speak with such candor that adults are often astonished. So it is in prayer, speaking candidly with God who affords individuals the opportunity to verbalize what God already knows. If children are to be taught to pray to God, they must develop a love for God. Children possess such great capacity to be awestruck; thus, children have the potential to develop a great love for God, become worshippers, and become people of prayer. Real prayer and communication come from love. How and why do children learn to pray? Children learn by observation, trying out words for themselves, imitating the words of others, and being allowed to discover the presence of God in their lives. The latter is perhaps the most significant and influential. While discovering who God really is, children begin to develop a relationship with God. Prayer grows steadily, slowly, hesitantly, with humor, honesty, and repetition as a trusting and loving relationship with God deepens.[2]

When adults take prayer seriously, children usually do also. Children soon sense if they are being asked to do something which parents or the significant adults in their lives do not value. In attempting to influence and encourage children to pray, it is most helpful for the parent or model to have a vital prayer life himself or herself. Modeling prayer and other Christian qualities help children to learn. Most parents' hope for their children is that the children would become moral, good, and loving people with a sense of their place in history. One of the main reasons parents give for offering religious instruction to their children in the area of prayer is so that the questions children have about the world, life, and death can be addressed. When children are taught to pray, they can begin to appreciate the fact that there is someone bigger than themselves or their concerns. Prayer helps to make children a part of the larger spiritual community. Parents and those who minister to children do well to understand that the basic religious instinct of children is a deep curiosity about why we are here. To discover that truth through prayer is worthwhile. Prayer offers children a standard of virtue, tradition, culture, and identity.[3]

Children seem to possess an intuitive spiritual sense and stand in awe of God. Children's early life experiences and exploration influence their concept of God and prayer. Imagery, thoughts, and feelings come together to make up what a child understands about God. The imagery, thoughts, and feelings are unique for each individual and are crucial to an understanding of God. This means that each prayer is unique because it reflects the love, worship, need, heart, and mind of that particular person. Children seem to have some of the same questions as adults have. Included in these are questions of faith, doubt, vengeance, power, justice, and love. Creating environments for children to freely speak of their understanding of God helps to foster the discipline of prayer. When afforded the privilege of developing their own ideas about God, children seem to exhibit a strong desire for personal relationship and communication with God.[4]

Prayer as an aspect of worship is an individual's response to God and that response may be in the form of communication (prayer). Prayer is usually based on a person's idea of God and children get their ideas from experiences with people (parents, teachers, caregivers). These experiences serve as a foundation for all learning and the child's most numerous and influential experiences occur in the home. A child's first prayer may be one of giving thanks. As children talk to God, they can easily identify people or things to thank God for (including parents/family, food, clothing, toys, or pets).

Other types of prayers may surface as a child grows and begins to develop a clearer and deeper concept of God. A recognition and understanding of what is right and good introduces children to the prayer for help and forgiveness. Prayer becomes a way of life for the child who grows up in a home and church where others talk with God. Prayer becomes a way to express love through communication with God.

Even the most superficial study of the prayer discipline shows that a certain basic structure is fairly obvious. That structure involves the first step of a distinct form of address. For example, "Holy Father", "God of our fathers", "Our Father", "O Lord" are all forms of address. These greetings usually express a sense of closeness or fellowship. This is precisely what is modeled when children are taught to recite and memorize the Lord's Prayer, beginning the prayer with "Our Father". Even though there is a sense of warmth and familiarity by calling God 'Abba', there is awe and wonder because of the one who receives the prayer. Feelings of fear and dependence may also surface. It may also be that in this greeting a recognition of God's relationship to the world will cause a person to reflect on God as Creator, Giver and Sustainer of life, Redeemer and Friend. In David Heller's findings, the first part of his interview with children dealt with naming the deity. To help determine the responses, children engaged in a drawing activity. These drawings help to define the one to whom prayer was offered. They were also helpful in naming the deity to whom the children prayed. Heller points out that drawings are excellent indications of the values and preferences of children since they show what is important to children as it relates to God and prayer. It is suggested by some researchers that drawings are advantageous tools, as they seem to dig deeper into the person, into his/her being.[5]

A mood of a close relationship that is modeled by Jesus in praying the Lord's prayer can lead into a natural feeling of expressing some form of thanksgiving and praise. Thanksgiving can inspire an awareness of shortcoming or failures and a deep desire for forgiveness. Experiencing this forgiveness might produce a cleansing process and a desire to change behavior. The next step will most likely be a sharing of one's needs, hopes, and desires with God who genuinely understands. Making one's individual request known extends to the fact that all of humankind has needs. Prayer can then be an opportunity to seek God's guidance as to how individuals can be empowered to impact their sphere of influence. Prayer is more than a pious ceremony or formality.[6] By providing opportunities that allow children freedom of expression, teachers can assist them in learning the language of prayer. There can be moments of spontaneity and creativity as it relates to praying. Polly Dillard writes, "Five year-old Sue touched the soft petals of the flower in her hand. She smelled the sweet fragrance. She stared at the bright yellow color. There was a feeling of wonder. Mommy said God made flowers. How could he? "Pretty flower," said Sue.

Making up her own melody, she sang a prayer of thanksgiving:

> *Pretty flower. Pretty flower.*
> *I like you.*
> *Pretty flower. Pretty flower.*
> *Thank you, God.* [7]

When methods such as memorization or recitation are used in teaching children how to pray, we offer them words for feelings they may not be able to fully express. If words do not come easily, there is silence in praying. Researchers have found that during meditation and other forms of religious contemplation, a sector of the brain becomes calmed. Using a brain-imaging machine, a group of Franciscan sisters in prayer were found to experience a calming in the 'orientation area' of the brain. This phenomenon may translate the experience of meditation into a feeling of oneness with God. Andrew Newberg of the University of Pennsylvania and Eugene D'Aquili, researchers in the newly emerging field of neurotheology, thinks human brains are "wired to encouraged religious beliefs". Newberg explains that the brain is set up in ways to help us survive and that religion offers the reassurance that there is purpose and causal effect in this scary world. In this way, religion and spiritual experiences are right in line with what the brain tries to do for us.[8]

Helping children develop the habit of silent prayers can provide them with a bit of peace even in the hurried lifestyles children sometimes lead. When children's bodies and mind are quiet and still, prayer might then be a natural result or outcome. Brother Lawrence suggests that we make a private chapel of our heart where we can retire from time to time to commune with God peacefully, humbly, and lovingly. His encouragement is to make inward prayer the last act of the evening and the first of the morning. It comes over a period of time and it is developed one step at a time.[9]

In the words of Laubach, "this sense of cooperation with God in little things is what astonishes me, for I have never felt it this way before. My part is to live this hour in continuous inner conversations with God and in perfect responsiveness to His will".[10]Kelly writes, "Life from the Center is a life of unhurried peace and power. It is simple. It is serene. It is amazing. It is triumphant. It is radiant. It takes no time, but it occupies all our time. It makes our life programs new and overcoming". Kelly tells us that "the wells of living water of divine revelation rise up continuously day by day hour by hour, steady and transforming. There is a way of ordering our lives mentally on more than one level at once. On one level we may be discussing, thinking, planning, calculating, meeting all the demands of external affairs and yet deep down on the inside, behind the scenes, be in prayer, song, worship, and praise. [11]

Howard Thurman writes that there is great virtue in the cultivation of silence. His suggestion is that each period of prayer should afford an experience of self-examination in the presence of God and in silence.[12]

One might ask the question, " Why is it important to encourage the development of this discipline called prayer?" One of the main reasons might be to examine the correlation between personal prayer and finding purpose in life. Prayer in life is a particularly rich concept explored both in psychology (Frankl 1978) and theology (Tillich 1952). Both emphasized that value and meaning of life is the chief motivation for helping people survive. It is the knowledge of the fact that one's life has meaning which helps an individual find purpose in life. This concept is understood to be central to the meaning-making process of life as opposed to meaninglessness. In the study of Francis and Evans, an exploration of the relationship between prayer and perceived purpose in life among a sample of twelve-to-sixteen-year-olds suggested that frequency of personal prayer may be an important predictor of the understanding of one's purpose in life. [13]

Thurman commented that a person wants to know that his life's purposes and plans are secured by a structure that is more than the individual. People desire this structure to be more significant and comprehensive than themselves. When this assurance is found and established, the sense of being adrift and living a meaningless life disappears. This assurance can be discovered in serious searching during prayer.[14]

Children are inherently inquisitive and naturally want to know the why, how, what, and when of things. The more they understand the 'why' of prayer, the more likely they are to do it. When a good learning environment (one that is attractive, clean, orderly, interesting, challenging, stimulating) is available, activities promote feelings and feelings may lead to prayer.

A group of five-year-olds worked busily making play-dough peas and potatoes for an imaginary meal. Mrs. Smith walked by as the children sat down to this meal.

"I am glad God sends the sunshine and the rain to help our food to grow," she commented. "God is good to help us have food to eat."

"At our house, we thank God for our food," remarked Jim.

"Sometimes, I get to do it."

" 'Thank you, God' are words in the Bible," said Mrs. Smith.

"Let's thank God now," suggested Jim. He closed his eyes and said a sentence prayer.

Mrs. Smith wanted other children to know about this moment of giving thanks to God in prayer and asked how might they let other children know about what happened.

"We could write a prayer," suggested one of the children.

"How do you suggest we do it?" asked the teacher.

"We could name the things we are thankful for", one of the children replied. *"We could use a Bible verse with what we name."*

"O give thanks unto the Lord for He is good" was chosen to use in the prayer with the things named by the children.

Working together, they wrote:
For our church and the people in our church
"O give thanks unto the Lord, for He is good."
For our preacher and our teachers.
"O give thanks unto the Lord, for He is good."
For our friends at church and school.
"O give thanks unto the Lord, for He is good."
For our fathers and mother and brothers and sisters.
"O give thanks unto the Lord, for He is good."

The prayer was used as a litany with the other boys and girls.[15]

Yearning to learn to pray is perhaps the entrance to a new stage in one's spiritual journey. This longing may be inspired or awakened by an admired person who is known to be a person of prayer. Apparently this was the situation with Jesus and His disciples who said, "Lord teach us to pray". [16]

This longing can be cultivated in children as they are encouraged to mediate, be silent, and imagine. What images come to their minds when children think about God? Do they see God as active in their lives? David Heller reported that, as children move from early to middle childhood, they shift from perceiving God as a close, personal friend to understanding God as a distant and powerful authority figure. He also reported gender differences in children's perceptions of God's involvement. Boys' and girls' categorizations of God seem to follow gender stereotype. Boys perceived God as distant, yet active, omniscient and rational. God was viewed as an organizer of projects and in control through indirect contact. Girls perceived a closer, more personal, passive God.[17]

God may be categorized in terms of gender and if God is perceived as male (possibly based on traditional biblical references to God as "He"), the relationship that children may have with their fathers can prove critically important for children's perception of God's nearness.[18]

Kirkpatrick and Shaver (1990) report that older children indicate a closer more involved God than did younger children. Children also indicated a closer, more involved God in situations requiring nurturing rather than judgement or punishment. As children move from early to middle childhood, they rely lesser on direct contact with parents. The parental attachment becomes internalized. This theory suggests that a need for attachment is life-long and that as children gain distance from parents, God is perceived as closer. In examining God's involvement in problematic situations and parental involvement, this model is supported. When parents are less involved and when children desire a nurturing figure, God is perceived as closer especially for girls.[19] These perceptions of God can have a tremendous influence on the practice of prayer. Roberta Bondi began to sort through her perceptions of her earthly father and her Heavenly Father during the second half of graduate work at Oxford. She admits, "I found that in public prayer, the very use of the name Father regularly filled me with a sense of inadequacy, helplessness, and depression." [20]

Since prayer is based on a relationship with God and all relationships include communication, it is important to have some knowledge of the most effective method of communication. Robert Coles writes of a conversation with a girl who said she prayed regularly and had periods of genuine piety. She would stop everything and give herself over to prayer (a habit she had learned from her mother and an aunt). The girl described the communication she has with Jesus by saying she goes into the quiet of the sunroom and thinks of Jesus. She begins to pray, not her 'regular' prayer, but something more like: " *Dear Jesus, I'm a little tired, and I can feel myself getting moody. And I'm not being 'charitable' the way they tell us in Sunday School, like you were. So please, if you can, help me.*" The little girl indicated that sometimes at the conclusion of her prayer she might resume her regular tasks. Other times, she might close her eyes and think of Jesus. She might even picture Him and hear Him saying, 'You have got to think of others, and not just yourself'. From this the child got the feeling that Jesus was on her side and understood what she was going through. Her response to this kind of exchange was one of gratitude as she reported, "I am sure grateful when I hear Jesus speaking. It is real helpful. I can remember what He said later, when I need to remember. I can be calm then and not goof up."[21]

This child's prayer illustrates Anderson's and Johnson's qualities of childness (it is the case for children and also adults). These four images include: (1) we never outgrow the vulnerability of childhood, even when we are no longer obviously small, weak, and needy. (2) the infinite openness of childhood is already an expression of mature religious existence. (3) the immediacy of being a child is what makes direct speech possible. (4) children teach us about dependence and neediness as inescapable dimensions of being human.[22]

In a response to the concept of God in prayer, one teen wrote, "I just feel, I just feel He is there. There may not be any material proof but I *know*. I can bet my life on it. Really. I know because He has talked to me." She explained that God talks with her in the form of feelings, feelings that God cares when she has struggled with a problem. On an occasion when one of her friends turned against her, she went into her room and cried. As she thought about her situation, she said, "Then I remembered that, you know, there was God and I just asked Him to tell me something, tell me what I could do."[23]

This kind of transformation is what can happen as a result of prayer. When individuals pray earnestly, they are on path to have every aspect of their lives taken over by God and changed. Children who form the habit of praying morning and evening are forming healthy habits. Developing the habit of praying daily is similar to developing the habit of brushing teeth, taking a bath, or taking vitamins each day. They help to keep one clean, get rid of that which might be harmful, and strengthen the soul. Prayers at bedtime can function as a bridge that transports a child from activity to repose, from excitement to calm, providing a way to become tranquil before falling into a peaceful sleep. These prayers can also be instrumental in encouraging a warm rapport between children and parents. Perhaps most important of all, these prayers can be a way to open and expand a child's heart, mind, and spiritual horizon in a helpful and happy way. By taking a few minutes each day to think of and pray for other people, a child develops the habit of being generous and loving. Prayer helps children reach way down inside themselves and way out beyond themselves. It can also help increase understanding of themselves, others, and the world in which they live. In this way children learn to be truthful in their prayers. They are not afraid to tell God how disappointed, angry, hurt, or upset they really are. Children learn that God is not shocked by what they say or feel. If children learn this, they will have a gift far more valuable than toys or jewels. Children will have a solid rock on which to stand all their lives. They can be confident no matter what happens in their lives. Children will have been taught a reliable technique for coping with both little and large problems. Prayer will show children a method to acknowledge privileges and joys with deep appreciation. Prayer is a way for a child to examine his/her personal goals and values creatively and thoughtfully. Children can have both roots and wings through the discipline of praying.[24]

The truth of discipline applies to prayer. Think of the accomplished pianist who may at present run his/her hands up and down the keyboard once had to agonize over the simplest scales. The task of prayer may begin as somewhat artificial, routine, simple, and conspicuous. Adults can teach children that everyday rote experiences can call them to prayer. For the student or teacher, it may be the ringing of the bell; for the surgeon, each scrub down, for the banker, each time a customer comes to the window. It could be whenever they feel the cool breeze, see the bright sunshine, or witness children playing. It might also be when they take a walk, stand in line, wash dishes, or clean. This work of prayer becomes more tender, more loving, more spontaneous, and more of a delight.[25]

Routine helps to offer children a sense of security and stability. Most children thoroughly enjoy routine whether it is arranging their toys a certain way, correcting parents when a minor detail is omitted from the favorite story, or being tucked into bed with a good night hug. Part of the routine can be to focus on the joy of prayer. If praying makes children happier, they will be more inclined to do it. Once children have been taught to enjoy prayer, they will be on the path of enjoying a happier relationship with the One to whom they pray.[26]

One of the routines in helping to teach children to pray is to write down the requests and God's answer. Howard Hendricks writes of a family who started a prayer notebook in which requests were recorded along with God's answers. God's answers could be 'yes', 'no', or 'wait'. One such story reviewed here is an example of God's 'yes'. During devotions this family would write down the requests. The father of the family had been a business owner, but felt compelled to enter into vocational Christian work. He sold the business, entered into the work He believed God called him for, and suffered financially. One night during the devotions, the youngest son asked, "Daddy, do you think Jesus would mind if I asked Him for a shirt?" The request was written in the book and to be sure the little boy made sure that his request was prayed for nightly. The entry read 'shirt for Timmy'-size 7. For four weeks they prayed, then one day the mother received a phone call from a businessman who was a clothier. He made mention that the July clearance sale was just completed and that he had something that they might need-boys' shirts. When the mother asked what size, the answer was 7. When she asked how many, the answer was 12. The family planned a ritual for presenting the shirts. That night during devotions when the boy reminded the family to pray, the mother told him that they could stop asking and that the Lord had already answered that prayer. The older brother went in and out of the room until all twelve shirts were piled on the table. This child was convinced that there was a God in Heaven who was interested in and cared about a boy's need for a shirt. The recording of prayer requests and God's answers is a simple, yet profound method of developing the habit of prayer.[27]

The desired end of the story of the little boy who faithfully prayed for a shirt and wrote his request may not be the end for every child. Writing the request and waiting to see what God will do is a very important lesson in prayer. Many times, the answers that God provides are so far above and beyond what we have imagined. Children are taught and can learn about patience. They also learn that not all requests are granted, nor is God magical. In teaching children how to pray, an understanding (or at least some familiarity) of the various theories of learning was helpful to me. Erik Erikson's outlines the stage of development 'trust vs mistrust' as a crucial psychological-social crisis for a child. As it relates to prayer, this stage is essential since the whole of Christianity hinges on faith and trust. Trust is an absolute necessity in prayer. Adults help children in their understanding of prayer to view the God in Whom they trust and the relationship with Him as more important than the desired answer to our request. It may often be that a greater benefit is gained when the prayer is not answered in the specific way that was initially requested. Home is a place where disappointments, doubts, and yes, even anger are lived out and acknowledged.

Children learn about the prayers of intercession as they consider others and their needs. Coles' account of a conversation with a woman who reminisced about her childhood experience illustrates this kind of prayer. The woman recalls an occasion in her childhood when her mother is explaining the dilemma of hunger in the world. As the mother explains this, the child is eating a doughnut and can not fully understand why other children in the world do not have food as she does. In the process of attempting to understand why other children can not have doughnuts, this little girl decided to help. Her thought was to give her doughnut to some child who had no food. The mother's response was that they could not simply do that because these hungry children did not live nearby. In retrospect, the woman remembers that she did not eat that doughnut, but rather put it on the table. This must have been a defining moment in the child's life as she remembers that her mother referred to it many years later saying that her daughter kept asking was there someone who needed her morning doughnut more than she did. She asked her mother if God knew someone nearby who could be fed from their abundance. Though the woman did not remember asking the mother about God's help in the matter, but her mother says she continued to talk about Jesus and God feeding the hungry.[28]

Children can begin to learn more about prayers of intercession if it is explained to them that this type of praying means they show God the person they love. This kind of prayer is surrender to God on behalf of another. It lifts the burden off our shoulders and puts it into God's hands. A surrender of the will is a requirement as the prayer is an act of giving over to God, rather than asking. Praying for others seems to be universal and a part of the depth of human nature. It can be equated to God setting up channels or paths for us to love and care for one another. Intercessory prayers are the means by which children are discovering and making a connection between other people and themselves. Children can be encouraged to pray for others, even those who treat them poorly. This is what Jesus taught in Matthew 5:44. This helps to view that person as God sees them. Sometimes one knows what effect his/her prayers can have on the person for whom he/she prays. [29]

In teaching children about intercession or praying for others, encourage them to use their imaginations. Just as an architect has a mental picture of the finished building he or she is designing, the child can have a picture of the person for whom he or she is bringing before God in prayer. To have a picture in one's mind of how things could be is very helpful in praying for others in that visualizing what is being prayed for offers a specific and desired goal. Children can be led into seeing a situation or a person change. This kind of prayer may be for a certain request or it could be asking God's love for the person. This is not an exercise in mysticism, but rather it is biblical even as Jesus told His disciples to picture moving a mountain into the sea (Mark 11:22-24). [30]

Intercession means that children are taught to go and influence the world from a place in prayer. Picture this, a young man is totally paralyzed. Two strong men lifted him and took him to the healing treatment of physical therapy. This is a symbol of what we do in intercession. We lift those we love to the healing presence of the Great Physician.[31]

Carol Zaleski cites one discovery of her son John as he ventured into the woods near a woodland chapel at a Benedictine monastery in Massachusetts. What he found was a carved sign and a bell on a tree. The sign read "St. Gertrude's". On closer examination, they saw a tent and Coleman stove, but no person who occupied that space. Later in the chapel during the monastic liturgy, they spotted an elderly distinguished-looking gentleman kneeling at his pew. Surrounding him was a row of photographs and a list of names including his wife and others for whom he prayed. The tent was this man's hermitage for that winter. Carol and her family imagined that the list of photographs and names of the people he loves go with this man creating a living picture of his ceaseless intercession. She viewed this as an experiment worth repeating, even if its final outcome will only be known in heaven.[32]

Children of all ages can be encouraged to enter into prayer with their whole and entire being. Prayer involves the spirit, mind, and body. The use of one's hands in prayer can help in creating an atmosphere for quietness and worship, praise and thanksgiving, or unity and oneness. When told to fold hands and bow heads, children may begin to understand this as preparation for prayer. It gives a sense of bodily quiet and expectation. Lying or kneeling suggest bowing before God in worship and adoration. This kind of body language communicates reverence and respect for God. Children can be taught that it is not just their mouths or words that say the prayer, but the entire body can be a part of the praying. Hands raised or waving can foster a sense of praise, celebration, and joy. Children can appreciate movement in prayer as they learn that Miriam and King David of the Bible dance. Holding hands in a circle during prayer demonstrates love and an unbroken kinship among those who pray. This practice helps all who participate to experience a sense of belonging which is essential for the readiness of the prayer practice. Children learn to show compassion and care for others by a touch. By introducing many body postures, children learn that the prayer life is full of variety and that the body is an integral part of prayer. Offering a variety of postures helps children to adopt several that may be appealing to them.[33]

Prayer is communicating with God showing one's thanks, love, hope, trust, faith, and dependence. Drawing and other forms of art provide children with a method to express all that is in their imaginations and to use their hands. In the process of picturing, children do some prayerful activities. They may pause to wonder. While drawing children often become quieted, restored, fulfilled and even surprised. To live as Christ lived is to be a prayerful presence in the world. Children learn prayers more heartily when they draw interpretations of phrases and then rewrite them according to their own images.[34]

Prayer for children can be explained as 'Thanks/Wow', 'Sorry-Oops', 'Please Help/God bless-gimme'. In helping children remember the things that they have or that they appreciate having, they can be encouraged to pray the 'Thanks/Wow' part of prayer. During these periods of reflection, everyone has some experiences when he/she does wrong, makes mistakes, and needs forgiveness. To sincerely check oneself daily allows for growth. This process often keeps one from being too prideful. This is the 'Sorry-Oops' part. In the checking up on oneself exercise, children and adults realize and recognize their need for forgiveness. 'Please help/God bless/gimme' represent the petition and asking part of prayer. It may be on the behalf of others or oneself that this part of the prayer is expressed. [35]

It is not out of character for children to ask God for the healing of a parent, grandparent, friend, other sick children, themselves, or pets. Children may have heard prayers for the sick in worship or they remember Bible stories in which prayers were offered for sick people. In addition to the spiritual benefit, there is growing evidence that prayer positively impacts the physical and mental health of humans, animals, and single cells. Findings of a study that examined the relationship of frequency of prayer on health outcomes in a national sample of 1,014 church leaders can be encouraging for those who practice prayer. The purpose of the study was to isolate the variable of frequency of prayer as an indicator of individual spirituality. In addition the purpose included examining the relationship of this variable to the eight subscales of health in the Medical Outcomes Study Short Form 36 Health Survey. What is the relationship of frequency of prayer to health outcomes in a sample of Presbyterian Church lay leaders or Ruling Elders was the research question. Researchers hypothesized that a higher frequency of prayer would be associated with better health. Sample population was randomly selected from the 2.6 million national population of the Presbyterian Church and asked to complete a series of questionnaires during a 3-year period from 1997-1999. Results indicate that prayer is a significant predictor of positive mental health. Nurses might apply these findings by recognizing prayer as a health practice that is helpful. They can pray. [36]

Prayer and children may both begin with primarily selfish motives in some instances. The thought of handing God a shopping list and then waiting for Him to automatically give whatever is asked is the description of self-centered praying. As people mature in faith, understanding, and prayer, they can begin to see things from God's perspective. Prayer becomes periods of time spent seeking what God plans are and how one can join in those plans. The focus of praying is then shifted from what God does for those who pray to what His followers can do to advance God's Kingdom. With this change of focus, praying people including children, then become participants with God. Even the youngest among God's people who pray are coworkers with God bringing about His perfect plan for the world. [37]

Children seem to possess a great capacity to love, wonder about, and commune with their Creator. Much of the research by David Heller and Robert Coles points out the depth of the curiosity children have as it relates to God. The various accounts of the conversations with children about their thoughts and feelings about God and communication with God through prayer were fascinating to me. These stories relay an earnest desire on the part of children to be in relationship with God. Creating an atmosphere conducive to the nurture of children's curiosity about God and allowing children to probe helps to develop faith, worship, and relationship. Imagination is a gift from God to all of us and in children this gift can useful in faith development. Because we have been made in the image of God, the mind and the imagination are a reflection of God. Imagination can help children learn to meditate as they imagine being in God's presence and having Jesus right beside them. Robert Coles' reports of the various conversations with children about God and prayer were amazing. These interviews illustrate the profound depth of the thinking children engage in as it relates to spiritual matters. To read some of the encounters with God that those children told of in their conversation with Cole was thought provoking and enlightening especially the ones who spoke of their sincere, lengthy, and pious prayer periods. These reports were so indicative of the pure innocence with which a child seeks God and the response of God when He is sought. The honesty and candor in these reports were remarkable and compelling.[38]

Chapter III

A group of 50 individuals who have consistently expressed a commitment to and interest in helping children learn about the importance of prayer in the Christian life were asked to participate in a survey. The population included teens, young adults, and adults ages 15 to 72. Participants represented various denominational affiliations and influences including Baptist, Methodist, Catholic, Episcopal, Assembly of God, Lutheran, and Non-denominational. The young adults and adults who participated in this study have ongoing involvement in the lives of children and youth as parents, grandparents, godparents, teachers, Sunday school teachers, youth/children ministry workers, pastors, mentors, and coaches. Individuals who were surveyed had as many as 43 years of experience and as little as half a year in their various roles and relationship with children/youth.

The survey was developed to determine 1) the relationship to children of the participants 2) what methods were used by the sample population to teach children how to pray? 3) from whom do children learn about prayer? and 4) what kinds of prayers do children most often pray (for whom/what)? The survey consisted of seven questions requiring short answer responses.

The first question asked about the capacity in which persons were associated with children and the number of years of that association. Other questions included in the survey were asked to determine for what or for whom do children most often pray, how do children learn to pray, and what methods have been used to enhance the discipline of prayer.

Although the total number of participants was very limited (50), there was variety of relationships. Parents represented the highest number of participants followed by teachers, Church school or Vacation Bible School teachers, mentors/friends, children's ministry workers, coaches, grandparents, child care providers, godparents, and extended family members (uncles, aunts, or cousins). There was a wide range of the number of years that the participants have been in relationship or associated with children. The longest period of time reported was 43 years with the shortest period of time being a total of 6 months.

Survey results indicated that 25 participants listed **parents/ family** as those for whom children pray most often. Second in the survey of what children pray for was school. Several other people and things that were on the list included: friends, safety and protection, healing, giving thanks, peace, needy people, things/situations that upset them, and deliverance from problems or difficulties. According to the survey, children learn to **pray by observing and modeling**. Ranked as number one (more than 15 times) , participants listed parents and family members as those who are observed and modeled most often by children as they learn to pray. Church leaders (pastors, teachers, children/youth ministry workers) were ranked as the second most observed and modeled by children as it relates to learning to pray.

Prayer is usually discussed in terms of spoken words; however, survey participants indicated other expressions of prayer. Silent prayer was listed 12 times as the way prayer is most often expressed other than spoken words. Other prayer expressions reported were: drama/music/art, body position, journals, sign language, and praying in an unknown tongue/language.

Children most often offer prayers of petition seeking God's blessings and help. Individuals who answered the survey questions listed numerous methods used to enhance the discipline of prayer. The number one method used for enhancing prayer was **modeling prayer**. Other methods were: join others for prayer, encouragement, Bible study on the topic of prayer, pray for others (intercede), teach special prayers (table blessing, The Lord's Prayer, holiday/ special occasion prayers), share God's answers to prayer, inquire about prayer (accountability), and Bible reading.

The methods for teaching prayer from the research and the expression of prayer from the questionnaire that were most similar were modeling prayer, memorization, writing, drawing/art, body movements/dance/drama. It was very evident from both that children learn best when they regularly witness living examples of persons who have a vibrant prayer life. The home environment is the most effective in establishing the prayer life of children. When children sense that prayer is practiced and is common place in the most central place of their existence (the home), there is a greater chance that prayer will be viewed as significant, foundational, and familiar. Often the home is where children are free to be fully themselves; so it is more likely that prayer when practiced in the home becomes a part of children lives. When children experience comfort with the idea of prayer, they are more likely to actually do it. Home is the first place one learns about communication and building relationships. Prayer has as its foundation a relationship with God and the relationship of children and their parents can have an influence on the child's understanding of a relationship with God. The home and parents are foundational to the discipline of prayer as with other habit-forming practices. Children imitate words and as a result speech is developed. Children mimic all kinds of behavior that they have observed from talking on the telephone to shaving, smoking, cleaning, or reading. Many of these imitations will be lifelong practices even before they are fully understood. Much of the research and the survey emphasized the important role of the home and family in developing prayer discipline. It is in the context of family that many occasions will arise that require prayer and children who learn early the practice of prayer are better equipped to meet the challenges of life. These challenges are in and away from the home. In most cases, since children will get most of their first ideas about God from the home, parents and other family members within the sphere of the home life have the opportunity and privilege of shaping the prayer life of a child early. When teaching a child about prayer and how to pray, one of the considerations to keep in mind is that the child is not too young to begin to learn about prayer. Children are learning many things even prior to birth and during infancy (i.e. how to recognize a parent's voice, cry to get their needs met, etc.). Babies interact with their environment and are learning from everything they see, hear, touch smell, and taste. Just as human learning occurs in stages so does spiritual learning.

As children learn to trust the parent(s) with whom they share daily living and as that parent/child relationship proves healthy, children will most likely have a better understanding of what it means to trust God in prayer. Usually children do not hesitate to share their concerns, tell their parents that they love them or that they are sorry. Children ask their parents for what they need or want. This is the pattern of prayer. Though children have personal potential for relating to God, they may get their first impression of a 'Heavenly Father' from an 'earthly father'. If the 'earthly father' is absent, uninvolved, or uncaring, children may find it difficult to relate in prayer to God the Father at the onset of prayer development. However, if children experience the warmth, security, and unconditional love of an 'earthly father', they may be more inclined to adopt the concept of adoring, worshipping, and communicating with an unseen Heavenly Father. Children learn how to talk, listen, and do things together in the home. Likewise in prayer, children learn to listen to and talk with God. Children develop and grow in all areas of life (physical, emotional, mental, and spiritual) in stages. Just as children learn that they do not have to be perfect in other areas of home life (i.e. washing car, baking cookies, reading, moping floor, washing windows, etc.), they learn that they do not have to pray perfectly either. It can begin in a very simple manner and many times it may be awkward. It is a progressive process whereby we learn by doing. In the home a routine of praying is crucial for establishing this habit. The habit of praying maybe morning prayers before the day begins (greeting God and seeking God's guidance), during the day (acknowledging Him in all areas of life), or at night (thanking God for the day, its events, and for a peaceful night's rest). Setting aside time daily for prayer helps children learn about routines and cycles. Geddes, author of *Children Praying*, writes of children being comforted by routines that are predictable and reliable. In our culture, it is of great benefit to have prayer as a comfort and as a release for our fears. These times of prayer need not be boring just because they are routine. Times of prayer can be exciting, refreshing, and encouraging. Children can be the ones to lead in prayers that involve the blessing of a meal, travel, healing, special gift, or other occasions. This method of teaching prayer allows children to practice and learn within the confines of comfort and encouragement.

Keeping a prayer journal or calendar is another method that was highlighted in the research, as well as, the survey results. When requests are written, this activity invites one to seek clarity about what is really being requested of God and what one is prepared to commit to change and do. Written requests and answers from God helps an individual to keep a record of what is being prayed for at that given time and how God sovereignly answers. It is a faith building tool that children can keep on file for use in times of worship, praise, and thanksgiving as they reflect and call to remembrance the faithfulness of God as they worship. When children write requests they are better able to chart their own spiritual growth and development because what dominates their conversations with God and the kinds of prayers that they pray are before our own eyes in back and white. Like prayer, journals can be very private. For the sake of respecting the child's privacy parents, teachers and others who introduce this method of prayer should remind children that they do not have to share from their journals. This is a communication between them and God. The entries may be simply words or phrases. Journals may contain letters to God or special prayers that the child has read or memorized. Children can be directed to their journal to express a wide range of emotions or experiences. Keeping journals is also an excellent method for helping children develop linguistic skills. This process is somewhat therapeutic and it helps to transfer the concern from the child's heart and mind to paper. In some way, this is moving the need or concern from one's own hands to God's. This is not done in the sense that an individual has no responsibility, but rather trusting God's answers and guidance even when things do not turn out the way one has planned. Journals can help children to be appreciative for all the answers God has so graciously given over the years. They are of particular comfort and encouragement to children as they review God's intervention in the desperate and urgent concerns of their lives and the lives of those for whom they pray. The journal can bring brings joy, tears, and laughter to children as they recall the circumstances surrounding those special prayer requests and answers.

When children are taught to say 'thank you', 'I am sorry', or 'I hope you feel better', 'let me help you' or 'forgive me', they can transfer that same language to prayer. Just as they thank a family member of friend for a much appreciated gift or gesture, they can learn to thank God for His many gifts including life, good health, family freedom, eternal life, food, toys, clothing, flowers, birds, protection, homes, and countless other blessings.

Daily activities and habits in the home afford many opportunities to incorporate prayer. Listed below are some general suggestions to introduce the prayer practice along with other daily routines.

SUGGESTIONS FOR TEACHING PRAYER IN THE HOME:

- Meal time prayer-ask a different child each morning/night to thank God for the meal and His provisions or ask each child to thank God for a particular aspect of the meal (i.e. *God, I thank you for dad grilling the hamburgers; Father, thanks for teeth so we can chew our food; Thank you, Lord for the sweet corn from our neighbors' garden*).
- Thank you prayer-During times of prayer invite each person to say/write a "thank you" for someone/thing for which they are especially appreciative.
- Spontaneous prayer-unscheduled expression of prayer (adoration, petition, thanksgiving, or confession (i.e. *Dear Lord, you are so wonderful; Dear God, thank you for allowing Bill's leg to stop hurting; Lord, forgive me for not wanting to share my toys; Lord, please keep my grandma safe as she walks on the ice*).
- Silent/Meditative prayer-create atmosphere for quite worship. Imagine the person/thing you want to talk with God about. (*designate a certain place/ chair/corner/ room with Bibles,*

books, pictures, paper, pencils, crayons; soft music).
- Intercessory prayer-collect pictures of family members, friends, community/world leaders, needy, homeless, war victims, ill, etc. (pray-silently, aloud, written) for each one and their needs.
- Word prayers/poems-use the letters in a word to offer thanks or petition (i.e.

> **D**-doodling on paper towels
> **A**-adored by us
> **D**-dear Lord, guide my dad's bus
>
> **T**-tall
> **R**-raising their branches to God
> **E**-evergreens
> **E**-every kind
> **S**-swaying in praise to their Creator)

In addition to learning how to pray in the home, children might be taught how to pray in school or church. Not every home is a refuge from distress and distractions. In fact, it may be the center of such and may not be the ideal place for introducing and nurturing prayer. In homes where prayer is not modeled, practiced, or taught, children may then learn this art outside of the home. Christian education in churches and schools offer ministry and play a vital role in helping children grow spiritually through prayer. Ideally, the teaching, practicing, and nurturing of prayer would be a partnership between home, church and school to offer this education to children, but realistically it may be only one of the three. In many instances, with the exception of Christian day schools, discussions of God and prayer are not allowed. Church leaders, Church School or Vacation Bible School teachers may be the models from whom children learn the art of prayer. Children can be given opportunities to pray aloud or silently in groups, classes, or one-on-one. For children who may have little or no experience with prayers, teaching that prayer is a way to tell God that we love Him is an excellent introduction. Today's children and youth are not always awe-struck and may need some prompting to become aware of the majesty, wonder, holiness, and overwhelming power of God. One method to help children experience the greatness of God would include the following steps:

- **STEP 1** – help children realize and recognize Who God is (read scripture passages that describe the wonder of God; take a walk and observe/show pictures/ video of God's wondrous creation; discussions/ brainstorming ideas)
- **STEP 2** – list names/descriptions for God (i.e. All Powerful God, Creator God, Loving Father)
- **STEP 3** – sentence prayers of adoration for God that reveal wonder and amazement (i.e. All Powerful God, thank you for keeping the stars from falling; Creator God, our little baby brother is here with us; Loving Father, thank you for giving the birds enough to eat).

Churches model prayer for children during worship services with formal prayers. These take the form of praise, thanksgiving, confession, and intercession. Children may hear prayers offered for the world, community, sick, elderly, hungry, family of God, schools and many others. Prayers from the Bible are often a part of Liturgy. Children can review, recite, personalize and memorize these prayers in the privacy of their prayer time thus adopting them as their very own.

Children experience learning prayer with music, drama, art and dance. The Psalms were written as songs and are often sung during worship. Including music in teaching about prayer is an excellent way to reinforce concepts. Some children have God-given talent as it relates to singing, reading and writing music so that prayers set to music is a joyful. Active is a common descriptive word for children and dance allows children the freedom to move and use their bodies. For the child who is a kinesthetic learner, this is an ideal approach to teaching prayer. Children sometimes understand feelings and attitudes through movements. Movements or dance can be very simple for the young child, as he/she is encouraged to create his/her own and express feelings freely. Liturgical dance has its roots in biblical times and is also very contemporary. These movements can be more complex depending on the age and ability of the child. Involving each child in creating his/her own movement is encouragement to create personal prayers. The following list presents several options for children to be active in their worship and prayer time.

SUGGESTIONS FOR MOVEMENT PRAYERS

- Praise-uplifted arms and head
- Smile-represent happy or blessed in a prayer
- Love-fold arms across the chest
- World-arms making large circling motion
- Repentance/confession-kneeling and bowed head
- Unity/fellowship-holding hands

Skits, drama, role-playing, and games are fun for children and it affords them to learn without a great deal of personal investing or unveiling. Selected prayers from the Bible are ideal for role playing (i.e. prayers of Daniel (Daniel 2:20-23); David (Psalm 51:1-12); Miriam (Exodus 15:1-5); Nehemiah (Nehemiah 1:5-11); Paul (Ephesians 1: 15-23); and Mary (Luke 1:46-55).

Children may find it interesting to pretend to be a Biblical character as they relive the past in the form of prayer experiences especially if it is an adventurous or perilous time. Teaching prayers of confession can be effectively demonstrated through role playing as children act out various behaviors that offend God or hurt others (i.e. lying, idolatry, gossiping, or disobeying). During the discussion following the presentation, these behaviors are clearly identified and prayers of confession can be written and/or offered.

Playing games serve a vital role in teaching children about life. Children learn about cooperation, responsibility, leadership, patience, and consequences as a result of games. Prayer is obviously a very serious matter, but it can be taught by games. For example, when taking a walk children can be engaged in a game of 'search' looking for things God has created and give thanks for what is discovered along the way. Learning other concepts (i.e. colors, alphabets, or numbers) along with prayer can be a game. Child is asked to pick a color, number, or alphabet from the box. Children who have a certain color or sequential alphabets/numbers are asked to say a prayer for someone else (intercession). Children learn the joy of praying when a method like games is used and are more inclined to remember the activity as fun and enjoyable. Use of a variety of teaching methods insures that more learning is actually occurring, reinforces the concept, and helps retention of that concept.

Drawing or painting prayers can be enjoyable and educational for children. Art is an excellent method to allow children individual expression especially for a child whose tendency is to avoid or limit verbal communication. In addition to sharing his/her prayer, it may also be an outlet for an otherwise ignored talent. Children can draw prayers of concern or thanksgiving. Children may chose to draw cartoons making this style of expression very happy or joyful. Some of the suggestions listed here can assist parents and teachers as they encourage children to share their thoughts, feelings and concerns in profound non-verbal expressions.

SUGGESTIONS FOR DRAWING PRAYERS:
- People prayer-encourage children to draw a prayer for relationships *(this might include family, school, church, sports, or friends)*.
- Creation prayer-draw things that God has created for us to enjoy *(i.e. animals, trees, birds, water, sky, and food)*.
- Feelings prayer-draw a picture to show how you/someone else might feel at certain times *(can be used after a Bible lesson-i.e. Jesus healing the blind man, raising Jarius' daughter from death, Jesus feeding the multitude with a little boy's lunch, etc.)*.
- Object prayer-Children write prayers in the outline of some pattern *(i.e. a cross can serve as the outline of an Easter prayer, the outline could be an open Bible, butterfly, fish, flower, etc.)*
- Gratitude prayers-draw a picture to show what you are thankful

for today *(i.e. family, Bible, toys, house, books, pets, friends, school, etc.)*

Memorization is another common method for teaching prayer. Some of the more traditional or historic prayers that are commonly used during worship services (i.e. communion, call to worship, offering, and benediction prayers) can be taught to help expose children to our Christian heritage, historical perspectives, and inclusion in the worship experiences.

SUGGESTIONS FOR MEMORIZING PRAYERS:
- Puzzle prayer-construct puzzle pieces with the words to a specific prayer. *(Instruct children to put the 'puzzle prayer' together. This is an excellent group effort project).*
- Chart prayer-use a large poster with the lines to a certain prayer, leave blank spaces for the children to fill in *(i.e. Praise God, from _____ answer- Whom all blessings flow...)*
- Share- a- prayer-after a time of study and review, ask one child/youth to recite the first line of the prayer. *(He/she then calls on another student to recite the next line. This procedure continues until the entire prayer is completed).*

Practicing the types of prayers in easy to remember formats is also a familiar method for teaching prayers. For example, prayers that include and focus on **A**doration, **C**onfession, **T**hanksgiving, and **S**upplication (**ACTS**) is one method of teaching prayer. Other acrostic for patterns of teaching prayer include **P**raise, **R**epent, **A**sk (for others), and **Y**ourself (**PRAY**); **P**raise, **R**everence, **A**doration, and **Y**ield (**PRAY**); **P**salming-read a prayer from Psalms, **R**econciling, **A**doring, **Y**ielding, **E**ntreating, and **R**ealizing-knowing that prayer is part of our lives at all times (**PRAYER**).

SUMMARY

In summary, parents, pastors, Church School teachers, youth ministry workers, and others who are interested and involved in the lives of children and youth are probably aware of the God-consciousness in them. When prayer is thought of as coming to God, The Father with thanks for something He has given us, seeking forgiveness for some wrongdoing, with a request, out of fear, or on behalf of someone else, prayer then is more easily understood and practiced. This kind of understanding of prayer is something children can related to and grasp. In this way, it is an achievable task to teach children how to pray. Prayer does not need to be formal or lengthy, but rather an ongoing, loving communication relationship with God. As children grow into a deeper understanding of God and faith, their prayers will reflect that growth. Changes will be evident in the prayer/spiritual life, just as they are evident in the physical, intellectual, and social development of children. Prayer can then be taught and encouraged.

As children learn about praying, they begin to discover and experience a connection with people from various cultures and time periods. Prayer has been passed on for many years. "The Lord's Prayer" has been translated into many different languages and Christians all over the world pray this prayer. This commonality connects children with others in a way that few practices can.

Children learn to pray most often by observing and imitating their parents, other family members, and church leaders. Churches and families can unite to assist children in learning how to pray.

The home environment serves as the cradle for teaching and modeling prayer. Churches can offer classes and training for adults, parents, and others to better appreciate the God-consciousness of children. It would be advantageous for all expectant parents who have even the slightest interest in spiritual matters to read those accounts and begin to recognize the great potential that children have for knowing God. Churches can help meet the parenting needs of their congregations when information about the spiritual capacity of children is discussed. Churches have the responsibility to teach children the critical discipline of prayer. More training as it relates to the spiritual capacity of children is essential for those who might minister to children. When adults are aware of the great spiritual potential children, teaching the discipline of prayer becomes a priority in the Church.

Other frequently used methods of teaching prayer are memorization, journal writing, drawing/art, and movements or dance. These methods are varied so as to meet the needs and individuality of children. A variety of teaching methods helps to create enthusiasm and effective results. Children most often pray seeking God's help for others and themselves. This petitioning is not the only kind of prayer children pray. They often engage in prayers of adoration, confession, and thanksgiving. God has created within children a vibrant spirit, unique characteristics, and special talents with which they can adore and worship Him in countless ways. When explaining what the kingdom of God is like, Jesus took a small child as a live object lesson. This comparison validates the worth of children and their place in the very kingdom of God. Jesus commands us to let the children come to Him. He chose to send the Savior for the people He so loved and Redeemer of the world in the form of small child who experienced the teaching and training during childhood. Perhaps this is most significant demonstration of God's perspective of the potential of children in His plan for the world.

ENDNOTES

[1] Mark Pollard, It's Prayer Time (California: Regal Books), 1979.

[2] Christopher Herbert, Prayers for Children (Ohio: Forward Movement Publication), 1993 p.8.

[3] Martha Fay, Do Children need Religion? (New York: Pantheon Book), 1993.

[4] David Heller, The Children's God (Chicago: University of Chicago Press), 1986.

[5] Heller, The Children's God.

[6] Thurman, Howard, Meditations of the Heart (Boston: Beacon Press), 1981, 25.

[7] Dillard, Polly. "Children and Worship." Review and Expositor (Spring 1983).

[8] "Hardwired for God?" U.S. Catholic, v. 66 no. 4, April 2001, p.11.

[9] Lawrence, The Practice of the Presence of God, Washington: ICS, 1995.

[10] Frank Laubach, Letters by a Modern Mystic, (Syracuse, NY: New Readers Press, 1979), p.23.

[11] Thomas Kelly, A Testament of Devotion, (New York: Harper & Row), 1941, pp.31, 35.

[12] Howard Thurman, Meditations of the Heart (Boston: Beacon Press), 1981.

[13] Francis, Leslie and Evans, Thomas The Relationship between Personal Prayer and Purpose in Life, Religious Education 91.1 (Winter 1996).

[14] Thurman, Meditations of the Heart.

[15] Dillard, Children and Worship.

[16] Edward Thornton, Lord, Teach Us to Pray, Review and Expositor 76.2. (Spring 1979).

[17] David Heller, The Children's God.

[18] Amy Eshleman and Jane Dickie, Mother God, Father God: Children's Perception of God's Distance, International Journal for the Psychology of Religion 9.2 (1999).

[19] L.A. Kirkpatrick and P.R. Shaver, Attachment theory and Religion: Childhood attachment, religious beliefs, and conversion. Journal for the Scientific Study of Religion. (Spring 1979).

[20]David Heller, The Children's God.

[21] Amy Eshleman and Jane Dickie, Mother God, Father God: Children's Perception of God's Distance, International Journal for the Psychology of Religion 9.2 (1999).

[22] L.A. Kirkpatrick and P.R. Shaver, Attachment theory and Religion: Childhood attachment, religious beliefs, and conversion. Journal for the Scientific Study of Religion.

[23] Roberta Bondi, Be not Afraid: Praying to God the Father, Modern Theology, 9.3 (July 1993).

[24] Robert Coles, The Spiritual Life of Children . (Boston : Houghton Mifflin), 1990.

[25] Herbert Anderson and Susan Johnson, Regarding Children, (Kentucky: Westminster John Knox Press), 1994, p.22.

[26] James Fowler, Stages of Faith, (San Francisco: Harper & Row), 1981, p.156.

[27] Joan Bel Geddes, Children Praying (Notre Dame: Sorin Books), 1999, p. 18, 24.

[28] Richard Foster, Prayer-Finding the heart's true home, New York: Harper San Francisco, 1992, p.52.

[29] Bel Geddes, Children Praying, p.25-27.

[30] Howard Hendricks A Shirt for Timmy, Fundamentalist Journal 4 no.11, 1985, pp.53-54.

[31] Robert Coles. The Spiritual life of Children, p. 326-328.

[32] Delia Halverson, Teaching Prayer in the Classroom, Nashville: Griggs Educational Resource, 1989, p. 15.

[33] Rosalind Rinker, Teaching Conversational Prayer, Texas: Word Books, 1970, 85-86.

[34] Rosalind Rinker, Teaching Conversational Prayer, Texas: Word Books, 1970, 85-86, 93-94.

[35] Carol Zaleski, Storming Heaven, The Christian Century, v.18 no 5, February 7-14, 20001, p.24.

[36] Rosalind Rinker, Teaching Conversational Prayer, p.118-119.

[37] Janaan Manternach and Carl Pfeifer, And the Children Pray, Ave Maria Press: Notre Dame, 1989, p. 137.

[38] Bel Geddes, Children Praying, p. 28; 40-42;45-47; 51-52

[39] Meisenhelder, Janice; Chandler, Emily, Prayer and Health Outcomes in Church Lay Leaders, Western Journal of Nursing Research, Sage Publications, Inc: no. 6 (October 2000), p. 706-716.

[40] Prayer Diary, Women's Aglow Fellowship, Washington: 1989, p.2

[41] Coles, The Spiritual Life of Children.

BIBLIOGRAPHY

Abernathy, David. *Understanding the teaching of Jesus.* New York: Seabury Press. 1983.

Anderson, Herbert and Johnson, Susan. *Regarding Children.* Kentucky: John Knox Press, 1994.

Anderson, Vienna Cobb. *Prayers of Our Heart.* New York: Crossroad. 1993.

Batchelor, Mary. *The Doubleday Prayer Collection.* New York: Doubleday, 1996.

Bel Geddes, Joan. *Children Praying.* Notre Dame: Sorin Brooks, 1999.

Bondi, Roberta. *"Be not Afraid"*, Christian Century, March 1996.

Coles, Robert. *The Spiritual Life of Children*, Boston: Houghton Miflin, 1990.

Collingsworth, J.B. *10-minute Devotions for Youth Groups.* Colorado: Group Books, 1989.

Cornwall, Judson, *Praying the Scriptures*. Orlando: Creation House, 2000.

Cosby, Clair G. *Junior High's a Jungle*, Lord. Pennsylvania: Herald Press, 1988.

Creach, Jerome. *Psalms*. Kentucky: Geneva Press, 1998.

Christenson, Evelyn. *A Time to Pray God's Way*. Oregon: Harvest House Publishers, 19996.

Eshleman, Amy and Dickie, Jane, "Mother God, Father God", International Journal for the Psychology of Religion, 9.2, 1999.

Fay, Martha. *Do Children Need Religion?* Pantheon Books: New York, 1991.

Foster, Richard. *Prayer: Finding the Heart's True Home*. Harper: San Francisco, 1982.

Francis, Leslie and Evans, Thomas. "Relationship between Personal Prayers and Purpose in Life'. *Religious Education*, Winter 91.1, 1996.

Fowler, James. *Stages of Faith*. San Francisco: Harper & Row, 1981.

Gnika, Joachim. *Jesus of Nazareth*. Massachusetts: Hendrickson Publishers, Zinc. 1997.

Griffith-Jones, Robin. *The Four Witnesses*. San Francisco: Harper Collins, 2000.

Hallam, Frank. *The Breath of God*. New York: Thomas Whittaker Bible House, 1985.

Halverson, Delia. *Teaching Prayer in the Classroom*. Nashville:

Abingdon Press, 1986.

Hardesty, Brian. *Closer to God*. Nashville: Abingdon Press, 1997.

Heller, David. *The Children's God*. Chicago: The University of Chicago Press, 1986.

Herbert, Christopher. *Prayers for Children*. Ohio: Forward Movement Publication, 1993.

Holy Bible. King James Version. Grand Rapids: Zondervan Publishing, 1994.

Jaki, Stanley. *Praying the Psalms*. Michigan: William Eerdman's Publishing Company, 2001.

Kelly, Thomas. *A Testament of Devotions*. New York: Harper & Row, 1941

King, Larry. *Powerful Prayers*. Los Angeles: Renaissance Books, 1998.

Kirkpatrick, L. A. and Shaver, P. R., "Attachment Theory and Religion". *Journal for the Scientific Study of Religion*, 29 (S 1990), p. 315-334.

Laubach, Frank. *Letters by a Modern Mystic*. New York: New Readers Press, 1979.

Lawrence, Brother, *The Practice of the Presence of God*, Washington, D.C.: ICS, 1995.

Matthaei, Sondra. *The God We Worship*. Nashville: Abingdon Press, 1993.

Maynard, Morlee. "God and I can talk", *Review and Expositor* 87, Fall 1990.

Manternach, Janaan and Pfeifer, Carl. *And the Children Pray*. Notre Dame: Ave Maria Press, 1989.

Meisenhelder, Janice and Chandler, Emily. "Prayer and Health Outcomes in Church Lay Leaders". *Western Journal of Nursing Research*, 22 no. 6, pp.706-716.

Mosley, Glenn and Hill, Joanna. *The Power of Prayer*. Philadelphia: Templeton Foundation Press, 2000.

Pollard, Mark. *It's Prayer Time*. Regal Books: California, 1982.

Prayer Diary, Women's Aglow Fellowship. Washington: 1989.

Rinker, Rosalind. *Teaching Conversational Prayer*. Waco: Word Book Publishers, 1970.

Smith, Judy. Teaching children About Prayer. California: Educational Ministries, Inc., 1988.

Thornton, Edward, "Lord, teach us to pray", *Review and Expositor*, Spring 1979.

Thurman, Howard. *Meditations of the Heart*. Boston: Beacon Press, 1981.

Tutu, Desmond. *An African Prayer Book*. New York: Doubleday, 1995.

APPENDIXES/CHARTS

CHILDREN MOST OFTEN PRAY FOR:

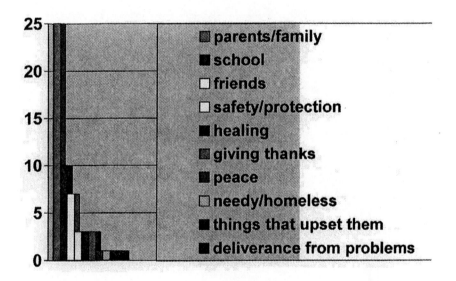

SURVEY PARTICIPANTS:
(relationship to/with children)

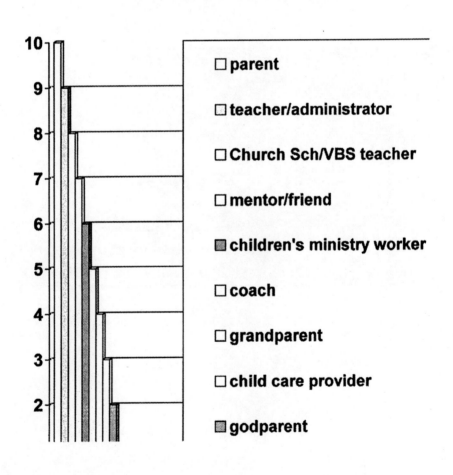

NUMBER OF YEARS
parenting/serving/teaching children

□ 43 □ 40 □ 35 □ 32 ■ 29

□ 25 □ 23 □ 20 ■ 19 □ 15

□ 13 □ 6 ■ 3 ■ 1 ■ 0.5

CHILDREN LEARN TO PRAY BY OBSERVING AND MODELING:

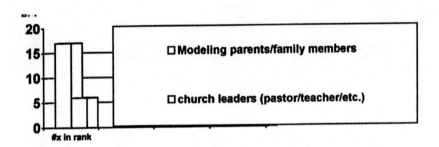

PRAYER EXPRESSION (OTHER THAN SPOKEN WORDS)

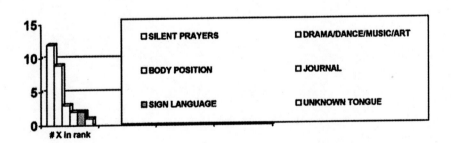

METHODS OF ENHANCING THE DISCIPLINE - PRAYER

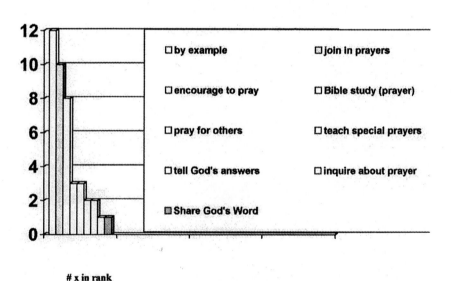

☐ by example   ☐ join in prayers

☐ encourage to pray   ☐ Bible study (prayer)

☐ pray for others   ☐ teach special prayers

☐ tell God's answers   ☐ inquire about prayer

☐ Share God's Word

x in rank

Printed in the United States
1276300001B/190-1143